THE
NATIONAL
ART
COLLECTIONS
FUND

Artfund100
1903–2003

MANY HAPPY RETURNS

THE NATIONAL GALLERY OF SCOTLAND CELEBRATES
ONE HUNDRED YEARS OF THE ART FUND

National Galleries of Scotland
Edinburgh · 2003

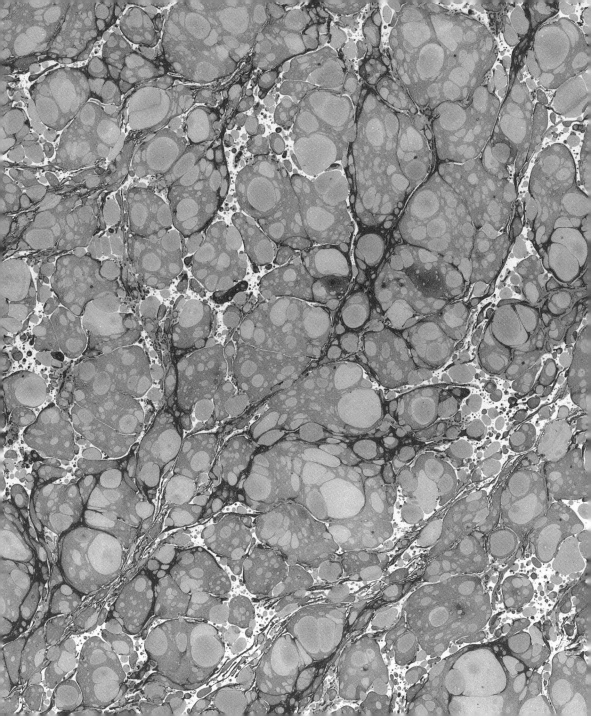

PAINTINGS & DRAWINGS

FROM THE NATIONAL GALLERY OF SCOTLAND
FROM RAPHAEL TO THE GLASGOW BOYS

The Wallace Collection
London · 2004

Published in 2003 by the Trustees of the National
Galleries of Scotland, Edinburgh, and the Trustees of
the Wallace Collection, London, on the occasion of the
exhibitions *Many Happy Returns: The National Gallery of
Scotland Celebrates One Hundred Years of The Art Fund*
held at the National Gallery of Scotland from 24 October
to 14 December 2003 and *Paintings and Drawings from the
National Gallery of Scotland: From Raphael to the
Glasgow Boys* held at the Wallace Collection
from 22 January to 18 April 2004.

© Trustees of the National Galleries of Scotland
ISBN 1 903278 47 3

Designed and typeset in Haarlemmer by Dalrymple
Printed in Scotland by Stewarts

Cover: François-Xavier Fabre, *Portrait of a Man*, 1809

FOREWORD

The National Gallery of Scotland has pursued a vigorous acquisitions policy in recent years, making spectacular purchases of works by artists of the calibre of Botticelli, Leonardo, Titian and Canova. But in the current climate, with limited resources and a remarkably buoyant art market, it could not possibly have managed this alone. The magnificent contribution made by the National Art Collections Fund (now called The Art Fund) has been a vital element in securing such successes.

We are delighted to have the opportunity to contribute to The Art Fund's centenary celebrations through this exhibition in Edinburgh, and to express our sincere thanks for all it has achieved. After being seen here, the exhibition will be shown in the spring of 2004 at the Wallace Collection, and we are most grateful to our colleagues there for making this possible. Our hope is that it will illustrate to a London audience the remarkable diversity of paintings and drawings in the National Gallery of Scotland, and inspire visitors to travel north and discover more of such a distinguished collection.

SIR TIMOTHY CLIFFORD
Director-General, National Galleries of Scotland

MICHAEL CLARKE
Director, National Gallery of Scotland

INTRODUCTION

When the National Gallery of Scotland opened its doors in the heart of Edinburgh in 1859, paintings from the neighbouring Royal Institution formed the nucleus of the works on display. They represented an eclectic collection that was relatively modest in scale. Since then the Gallery has evolved into one of the finest in the world; it is now renowned for the outstanding quality of its paintings and drawings, which provide a survey of many of the highpoints of European and Scottish art. This transformation was, however, slow to come about, as the Gallery depended on gifts and bequests, and initially had no government funding for acquisitions. By the late nineteenth century, this lack of resources became a matter of serious concern as opportunities for acquiring major works passed by, prices began spiralling upwards, and the spending power of overseas institutions and collectors increased. However, in 1903 two important initiatives helped to alleviate the problem: the Gallery was given its first annual purchase grant, and the National Art Collections Fund (NACF), or The Art Fund as it is now known, was founded.

The Art Fund is a charity supported by public subscriptions, and over the last one hundred years it has assisted with the purchase of numerous paintings, drawings, prints and sculptural works for the National Gallery. The extent of its success could hardly have been foreseen in 1903, but its influence has been so pervasive that a visitor to Edinburgh today can admire pictures by Velázquez, Claude, Constable and Nasmyth, sculptures by Bernini and Canova, and drawings by Leonardo, Raphael, Poussin and Ingres – all of which have been acquired with its help. Botticelli's *Virgin and Child Adoring the Sleeping Christ Child*, which was bought in 1999, was supported with the largest grant ever made by The Art Fund. Generosity on a similar scale has also made possible the acquisition of pre-eminent works for the Scottish National Portrait Gallery and Scottish National Gallery of Modern Art.

Such an achievement is remarkable in view of The Art Fund's origins. It was founded by a small and diverse band of enthusiasts (ranging from the Archbishop of Canterbury to the art critic Roger Fry), who sought to slow down the seemingly unstoppable export of works of art, and assist British collections with limited resources. Connections with Scotland were strong from the outset, as the first Chairman of The Art Fund was the Earl of Crawford and Balcarres. By the time of its inaugural meeting, which was held at Burlington House in London in November 1903, 296 members had been recruited. A century later membership exceeds 80,000.

The Art Fund contributed to the growth of the National Gallery's collection in a number of different ways. There have been paintings purchased outright which have been given to the Gallery, including works such as Cotman's *Buildings on a River* and Perugino's *Four Male Figures*, presented in 1905 and 1934 respectively. It has also provided a mechanism through which gifts and bequests of works of art are made, such as William Blake's dramatic watercolour in this exhibition, *Job Confessing his Presumption to God who Answers from the Whirlwind*, which was presented via The Art Fund in 1949. In addition, it has made possible important joint endeavours. In 1991 when a group of British museums and galleries formed a consortium to acquire old master drawings from the Holkham collection, The Art Fund provided critical assistance (as a result a small group of superb drawings came to Edinburgh).

However, it is, above all, by directly giving grants to support individual acquisitions that it has consistently played a vital role, especially as complex funding packages, which combine finances from a number of different sources, are now required to secure major works. An offer of money from The Art Fund has become a sign of approval and quality, and can stimulate further support; it was a key element in the recent acquisition by the National Gallery of Scotland of Titian's beautiful *Venus Anadyomene*. As well as making possible such high profile acquisitions, The Art Fund has on numerous occasions also helped to enrich Scotland's collections with important works by less well-known artists; these include the fine Danish paintings, nineteenth-century French pictures and ornament prints in the current exhibition.

Since 1903, special events have been organised to inspire contributions and engage people with The Art Fund's objectives. To mark its tenth anniversary the Earl of Ellesmere arranged a private view of Bridgewater House in St James's, which contained his family's splendid art collection. The paintings that could be enjoyed by members on that day, included works by Raphael, Titian, Poussin and Rembrandt – all of which have been on loan from the Ellesmere Trustees to the National Gallery of Scotland since 1945.

This small exhibition marks another special anniversary and forms part of countrywide celebrations. These provide an opportunity to thank The Art Fund and its members and inspire the continuation of their work. When the exhibition travels to the Wallace Collection in London, it will, in addition, illustrate the extraordinary variety and consistent quality of the paintings and drawings that the National Gallery of Scotland has acquired.

CHRISTOPHER BAKER
Chief Curator, National Gallery of Scotland

LEONARDO DA VINCI 1452–1519
Studies of a Dog's Paw [recto]

Leonardo was driven by an unrelenting curiosity about the appearance and structure of all aspects of the natural world. The extent of his studies are revealed in his notebooks, where drawings of landscapes, weather, water, plants, animals and human physiognomy appear in abundance. Some of these sketches inform his paintings, while others are related to independent research. This double-sided sheet, of which only the recto is displayed, falls into the latter category. It is filled with a series of incisive descriptive studies of the left forepaw of a domestic dog, which was possibly a deerhound. Typically, Leonardo does not simply study his subject from a single viewpoint, but extensively analyses it in an empirical fashion. The style of this impromptu drawing suggests it was made in about 1480, while he was working in Florence, and just before his departure for Milan.

The sketch is preserved in a richly ornamented sixteenth-century frame with a bar running across the top, from which, originally, a small protective curtain would have hung. At the lower left of the sheet of paper is a feint 'TL' stamp which signifies it was owned by the great Regency portraitist Sir Thomas Lawrence, who built one of the largest private collections of old master drawings ever assembled in Britain.

Metalpoint on paper coated with a pale pink preparation · 14.1 × 10.7cm · D 5189
Inscribed in black chalk at lower right of recto:
Leonard de V
Purchased by Private Treaty with the aid of the National Art Collections Fund 1991

[EDINBURGH ONLY]

RAPHAEL 1483–1520

A Kneeling Nude Woman with her Left Arm Raised

Raphael excelled at creating exquisitely controlled life drawings in preparation for his painted compositions. Here he can be seen planning part of one of his greatest Roman commissions: the fresco cycle in the loggia of Agostino Chigi's villa beside the river Tiber, which was completed in 1518. Chigi was a fabulously wealthy Sienese banker, an important papal adviser, and one of Raphael's most significant patrons. His villa was essentially a pleasure pavilion and the ceiling of the loggia was decorated with episodes from the lives of the mythic lovers, Cupid and Psyche. Raphael's kneeling woman is related to a scene of the *Toilet of Psyche*, intended for one of the frescoed lunettes, but not in fact executed; its composition is, however, recorded in a later print. This shows that had the woman been painted, she would have been depicted clothed, in the attitude of a handmaiden offering a dish to Psyche who was seated to the right. The partially drawn face and hands are probably for one of the other attendants who would dress the hair of the goddess.

Red chalk was first widely used in the early sixteenth century, and could be employed to create precise, descriptive outlines and model form with great subtlety. Both effects were brought to an extraordinary pitch in this consummate study.

Red chalk and touches of black chalk over traces of stylus underdrawing on paper · 27.9 × 18.7cm
D 5145
Purchased by Private Treaty from the Trustees of the Chatsworth Settlement, with the aid of the National Art Collections Fund, the National Heritage Memorial Fund, and the Pilgrim Trust 1987

AFTER POLIDORO DA CARAVAGGIO 1492–1543
BY AEGIDIUS SADELER I *c.*1570–*c.*1609

Design for a Vase

Just before the Sack of Rome in 1527, Polidoro da Caravaggio, who was one of the most accomplished of Raphael's pupils, decorated the façade of the Palazzo Milesi in the city with a series of mono-chrome frescoes, depicting classical scenes, trophies and vases. The wit and invention, particularly of the designs of the vases, meant that these motifs became widely admired, and their fame spread as a number of series of prints reproduced them. The first of these were created by Cherubino Alberti in 1582. This engraving comes, however, from a set published in Prague in 1605, which reverse the Alberti prints. The perspective of the vase is distorted, so it is seen as though in situ, and looked up at from street level.

The vase is one of 197 ornament prints acquired from the Birmingham Assay Office, which represented a major addition to the National Gallery of Scotland's graphic collection. These works included French, German, Italian and Netherland-ish woodcuts and engravings dating from the sixteenth to the nineteenth centuries. They were assembled early in the twenti-eth century as a resource for jewellers and silversmiths – and so until very recently served their original function as a means of transmitting imagery in a form that would inspire practising artists and craftsmen.

Engraving on paper · 24 × 16cm · P 2911.159
Purchased by the Patrons of the National Galleries of Scotland with the aid of National Art Collections Fund 1995

POLYDORVS DE CARAVAGIO. IN.

2

ROMÆ

DENYS CALVAERT c.1540–1619

The Holy Family with the Infant St John the Baptist in a Landscape

Calvaert was born in Antwerp, but travelled to Italy in about 1560, where he remained for the rest of his life, and chiefly worked on religious commissions. In Bologna he played an especially important role as a teacher for the next generation of Italian artists: Guido Reni, Francesco Albani and Domenichino were among his pupils.

This is a characteristic example of Calvaert's small devotional paintings, of a type that he produced in large numbers. It is closely related to a similar work in the National Gallery in Warsaw, and is thought to date from the period c.1590–1600. The Holy Family is accompanied by the infant Saint John, at the lower left, who holds a reed cross and receives Christ's blessing. They are at rest during the Flight into Egypt, and attendant angels provide fruit and spring water to sustain them. Above the mountainous landscape, a premonition of Christ's Passion appears: putti carry the cross and nails and the column on which he is to be scourged.

The smooth sheet of copper provided an ideal surface upon which to depict such a detailed and richly coloured design. According to Calvaert's biographer, Malvasia, his works of this type feature a 'singularity of thought, abundance of figures, distinct and well arranged expressions of emotion [and] grace'.

Oil on copper · 42 × 32cm · NG 2447
Purchased with the aid of the Patrons of the National Galleries of Scotland and the National Art Collections Fund 1987

GIULIO CESARE PROCACCINI 1574–1625

The Virgin and Child with the Infant St John the Baptist and Attendant Angels

Procaccini, although relatively little-known outside Italy, was one of the most successful and prolific painters of the early years of the seventeenth century. He was born into an artistic family in Bologna, which moved to Milan in the mid-1580s. His earliest works were statues commissioned for churches in Milan and Cremona, but in about 1600 he turned to painting. He worked across much of northern Italy, finding employment in Modena, Cremona, Pavia and Genoa, where he assimilated a broad range of styles.

This lyrical, small-scale devotional picture would have been intended as an aid to prayer and contemplation: it shows the infant Saint John holding up a lamb before the Holy Family, representing Christ's future sacrifice. Its style reflects Procaccini's study of Parmigianino's works, and it is painted with a liquid freedom usually associated with preparatory sketches, although it is considered a resolved painting. It has the distinction of almost certainly being the earliest work by the artist to enter a British collection, as it was owned by King Charles I. When sold in 1649, following Charles's execution, it was valued at five pounds, although realised seven. It later passed through the collection of the soldier-connoisseur, General John Guise, most of whose paintings and drawings were bequeathed to Christ Church, Oxford in 1765.

Oil on panel · 51 × 36.5cm · NG 2647
Purchased with the aid of the Heritage Lottery Fund and the National Art Collections Fund 1995

JOHANN KÖNIG 1586–1642
Angels Escorting Lot and his Family from Sodom

König was the son of a goldsmith from Nuremberg. He trained in Augsburg and then travelled to Italy, where he probably visited Venice before settling in Rome (1610–1614). It is there that he briefly came to know Adam Elsheimer, another German artist resident in Italy, whose influential jewel-like paintings on copper had a significant impact on his work. After returning to Augsburg, König was appointed dean of the city's painters' guild in 1622, and went on to fulfill a number of important municipal commissions. He remains best known, however, for his miniatures and cabinet paintings, which, with their insistent colours and multiple light sources, draw heavily on the precedent of Elsheimer's work. This example formed part of a series in which he depicted Old Testament subjects. Here, Lot and his daughters are led from the burning city of Sodom (Genesis 19), which König has imagined as being dominated by Italian buildings; for example, the porch at the lower right is based on that of the church of ss. Luca and Martina in Rome.

This drawing was an especially appropriate acquisition for the National Gallery of Scotland as the collection contains major paintings by Elsheimer. Its purchase commemorates the distinguished career of Keith Andrews, a noted Elsheimer scholar.

Gouache on paper laid down on panel
11.4 × 17.4cm · D 5137
Purchased with the aid of the National Art Collections Fund and contributions from two private donors, to mark the retirement of Keith Andrews as Keeper of Prints and Drawings at the National Gallery of Scotland 1985

NICOLAS POUSSIN 1594–1665

A Dance to the Music of Time

This important compositional study, which dates from the mid-1630s, is the only known preparatory drawing for Poussin's painting called *A Dance to the Music of Time*, in the Wallace Collection, London. The picture was commissioned by Cardinal Giulio Rospigliosi, who later became Pope Clement IX. According to Poussin's earliest biographer, Bellori, it was Rospigliosi who defined the subject (a 'moral poem'), which is an allegory about fortune and the cycle of human life, in which the dancers personify poverty, labour, wealth and pleasure. They follow the music of Father Time, who plays a lyre, while putti toy with an hourglass and blow bubbles (both emblems of life's brevity), and the Janus figure looks to the future and the past. In the sky, Apollo and Aurora emerge from the zodiac to herald the dawn, and the passage of the day and the year.

For Poussin drawing was a practical necessity, rather than a source of delight; this is, however, one of his most appealing studies, in which the sensual figures are defined as slightly abstracted forms, consistently lit from the upper left, as they appear to cavort upon a stage. In the painting the composition becomes more austere and measured. The title now used for it is a creation of the twentieth century, and has become widely known as it was adopted for a famous series of novels by Anthony Powell.

Pen and brown ink and traces of black chalk on paper · 14.8 × 19.9cm · D 5127
Purchased by Private Treaty with the aid of the National Art Collections Fund (Scottish Fund), the Pilgrim Trust, the Edith M. Ferguson Bequest, and contributions from two private donors 1984

[LONDON ONLY]

GOFFREDO WALS c.1595–c.1638
Landscape with Christ and St Peter

Although modest in scale, this type of painting is of great importance as an early example of a work dominated by a landscape, which heralded a new interest in such subject matter. Wals was born in Cologne and travelled to Italy, where he initially settled in Naples, and found employment colouring engravings. He later emerged as a landscape specialist, working in oil and gouache, and painted in Rome, Genoa and nearby Savona. He studied with Agostino Tassi, but is chiefly remembered because he taught the greatest of all French landscape painters, Claude Lorrain, whose ability to create harmonious compositions, must in part be indebted to the precedent of Wals.

Wals is thought to have died in an earthquake in Calabria. Although his work was admired during his lifetime and is recorded in distinguished collections, it was neglected by art historians before being re-evaluated from the 1960s onwards. He favoured small circular landscapes (other examples are in the Ashmolean and Fitzwilliam Museums) and a subdued palette, often paring the composition down to a series of distinct horizontal planes. The figures in this painting may be intended as Christ and Saint Peter, although the identification is by no means certain. The building is possibly the Tor di Quinto, a structure Wals depicted in other works, which survives by the river Tiber, near Rome.

Oil on copper · 28.5cm (diameter) · NG 2516
Purchased with the aid of the National Art Collections Fund 1990

SEBASTIANO RICCI 1659–1734

Christ Healing the Blind Man

Christ described himself as 'the light of the world' and restored the sight of a man who had been blind since birth, by annointing his eyes with clay (John IX). The miracle is depicted here as being observed by a soldier, a cripple, and a young mother, as well as the Apostles and Pharisees, whose expressions register belief and scepticism. As befits a painting about the gift of sight, it is sumptuously coloured and the complex architectural setting creates rich visual interest. These characteristics are, however, common to many of Ricci's works, particularly because of his admiration for the festive art of Veronese, which he studied during his training in Venice. As well as assimilating such sources, Ricci also adopted ideas from Roman and Bolognese Baroque painting.

He enjoyed an international reputation and travelled extensively, working in Parma, Rome, Florence, Vienna and London. During Ricci's years in England (1711/12–1716) he was employed by a number of important patrons, such as Lord Burlington and the Duke of Portland. This work is first recorded in the collection of Dr Richard Mead, King George II's physician, and as its subject is concerned with healing, it may well have been a gift to him from a friend or patient. Mead's collection also included paintings by Holbein, Ribera, Rubens, Panini and Watteau.

Oil on canvas · 52 × 67.5cm · NG 2623
Purchased with the aid of the National Art Collections Fund 1994

GEORGE ROMNEY 1734–1802
Study for 'Elizabeth Warren as Hebe'

Romney was born in Lancashire and trained as a cabinet-maker before turning to painting; after visits to Paris and Rome he established himself as a fashionable portraitist in London, rivalling Joshua Reynolds and Thomas Gainsborough. He developed a distinctive style of draughts-manship, often employing swathes of dark ink to establish the main features and key accents of light in his paintings. This impressive drawing is related to a portrait of Elizabeth Warren (National Museums and Galleries, Cardiff), commissioned by her father, which shows her at about the age of sixteen, just before her marriage to Viscount Bulkeley. It was the first major portrait Romney worked on after his return from Italy, and he made a number of preparatory studies for it, carefully refining his ideas. Hebe, an ideal personifi-cation of youth, was the cup-bearer of the gods, and in the final work Romney depicts his sitter before a cascade, with a vase before her, and an eagle, representing Jupiter, ominously hovering above.

Sir Edward Marsh bequeathed a number of important drawings to the National Gallery of Scotland. He pursued a distinguished career, which included a period working as private secretary to Winston Churchill, and also wrote books on poetry, notably a memoir of Rupert Brooke.

Pencil, ink and wash on paper · 38 × 21.5cm
D 4649
Presented from the collection of Sir Edward Marsh through the National Art Collections Fund
1953

WILLIAM BLAKE 1757–1827

Job Confessing his Presumption to God who Answers from the Whirlwind

Blake stands alone in the history of British art; his paintings, prints and poetry evoke a private world of religious, mythic and philosophical themes of searing originality. He pursued some conventional training as an apprentice engraver, and briefly as a student at the Royal Academy Schools, but persisted throughout his life with his unorthodox vision. One of the few contemporaries who admired his work was the military clerk Thomas Butts, to whose son Blake gave engraving lessons, and for whom he created over eighty works between 1800 and c.1809. They treated themes such as the Passion, Apocalyptic beasts and the Old Testament Book of Job, and this watercolour, which dates from 1803–5, is one of the most splendid.

Blake re-visited the subject of Job on a number of occasions (twenty-one of the watercolours bought by Butts explored it), possibly because he identified with Job's trials. Job steadfastly refused to abandon his faith in spite of the numerous misfortunes he had to endure, which included the death of his children and the destruction of his home. Here, at the climax of his torment, surrounded by his prostrated wife and friends, he experiences a mystic vision of God, who, with outstretched arms, is seen amid a vortex of angels. Light appears on the horizon, and Job will be granted redemption.

Pen and ink and watercolour over pencil on paper
39.3 × 33cm · D 2117
Signed, lower left: *W B inv.*
Presented by the Trustees of Mr Graham Robertson through the National Art Collections Fund 1949

ALEXANDER NASMYTH 1758–1840
A View of Tantallon Castle with the Bass Rock

Sir David Wilkie described Nasmyth after his death as the 'founder of the landscape painting school of Scotland'. He came from a family of artists and succeeded not only as painter, but also as a landscape gardener and engineer. He initially trained under Alexander Runciman, before working with Allan Ramsay, and then established himself as a successful portraitist in Edinburgh. In the 1790s Nasmyth developed the landscape style for which he is best known, which invariably involved integrating topographical details of country houses and castles within a picturesque context.

He is recorded as having exhibited three paintings of Tantallon, in addition to this especially dramatic, almost operatic, view, which is thought to date from *c*.1816, and is one of the finest of his maritime pictures. A related drawing of a shipwreck is in the collection of the National Gallery of Scotland. It is probable that he chose to treat the subject because the fourteenth-century Tantallon Castle, which is located outside North Berwick, was so memorably described in Sir Walter Scott's epic poem *Marmion*, along with a 'gathering ocean-storm,' (Nasmyth provided numerous illustrations for collected editions of Scott's poems). He also uses it, however, to explore a type of romantic coastal scene most readily associated with the great mid-eighteenth-century French painter, Claude-Joseph Vernet.

Oil on canvas · 92 × 122.3cm · NG 2627
Inscribed and signed with initials
Purchased with the aid of the National Art Collections Fund 1994

FRANÇOIS-XAVIER FABRE 1766–1837
Portrait of a Man

Fabre was a pupil of Jacques-Louis David in Paris, but spent much of his career in Italy: from 1787 in Rome and then from 1793 in Florence, where he was particularly connected with the English expatriate community. He specialised in half-length society portraits; their crisp design and minute attention to detail were largely inspired by David's paintings. He gradually produced a wider range of works, painting history pictures and landscapes, and was also active as a dealer, printmaker and enthusiastic collector. It is, above all, for his collection rather than his paintings that he is now best known; it is housed in the Musée Fabre in his native Montpellier and includes a number of important sixteenth- and seventeenth-century Italian paintings, as well as a wide selection of the artist's own work.

Fabre returned briefly to Paris (1809–10) and this intense and sensitive portrait of a fashionably dressed young man is dated to the first year of this visit. It bears a pencil inscription on the unpainted edge of the canvas: *M Camille*, which is presumably a reference to the as yet unknown sitter. His dishevelled hair is arranged in the so-called 'à la Titus' antique style which was then in vogue.

Oil on canvas · 61.5 × 50cm · NG 2548
Signed and dated 1809
Purchased with the aid of the National Art
Collections Fund 1992

JOSEPH MALLORD WILLIAM TURNER 1775–1851
Heriot's Hospital, Edinburgh

Heriot's Hospital, seen through the chaotic urban sprawl of early nineteenth-century Edinburgh, appears as an imposing although indistinct silhouette at the centre of this watercolour. Founded through a bequest to the city made by George Heriot (1563–1624), it was a charitable institution dedicated to the education of the orphans of freemen. The hospital, which is a magnificent example of Scottish Renaissance architecture, opened in 1659: today it houses George Heriot's School. The street in the foreground was the West Bow (now Victoria Street), a steep wynd which ran from the Old Tollbooth Jail down to the eastern end of the Grassmarket.

Turner composes the scene, which he worked on in *c*.1819, like a stage set, and contrasts the grand backdrop of the hospital with the crush of tenements and shops to either side. He takes considerable interest in the figures in the foreground, which include street traders, pedlars, and a group pushing a cart of coals uphill, many of whom wear tartan plaid. Particular care has also been taken over the jumble of objects at the right. Near them is a sign which appears to read 'English School' – this may be intended as an ironic reference to Turner's status as an English artist visiting Scotland.

Watercolour on paper · 16.6 × 25cm · D 5447
Purchased with the aid of the Heritage Lottery Fund and the National Art Collections Fund 1988

THOMAS GIRTIN 1775–1802
The Village of Jedburgh, Roxburgh

Girtin travelled to Scotland in 1796, making a brief sketching expedition in the Borders. He drew a panoramic pencil sketch of Jedburgh (The British Museum) which was used as the basis for two watercolours: one in a private collection, and this work, which was created four years later in his studio. The village is viewed from the vantage point of the site of its castle, looking towards the north. Girtin has omitted the ruins of medieval Jedburgh Abbey, which could be seen if the view extended further to the right, and uses the curve of the broad street to lead the eye towards the meandering river Jed in the distance. By excluding the Abbey he has shifted attention from Jedburgh's most famous landmark to the picturesque attraction of more modest buildings. The range of colours is relatively limited, but his ability to record texture is remarkable. The thatched roofs and wattle and daub walls of the houses are defined with great care as the late afternoon light gently rakes across them.

Girtin, like his friend and contemporary Turner, played an important role in heightening the status of watercolour painting. In the 1790s he developed works of extraordinary technical sophistication, most notably for Edward Lascelles at Harewood House. His career was, however, tragically curtailed by his premature death, possibly from asthma.

Watercolour over pencil on paper · 30.2 × 52.1cm
D 5175
Signed and dated in brown watercolour, lower left corner: *Girtin 1800*
Purchased with the aid of the National Heritage Memorial Fund, the National Art Collections Fund, and the Pilgrim Trust 1988

JOHN CONSTABLE 1776–1837
View on the River Severn at Worcester

Constable's pencil drawings are far less well-known than his oil sketches and large scale, highly finished paintings, but as intimate studies created in the open air they provide compelling evidence of how he immersed himself in study of the English countryside. This fine example, which is enlivened by details such as the abandoned barges and horse drinking at the water's edge, illustrates the breezy naturalism and compositional clarity he was able to convey, even in such modest works.

Constable is chiefly known for his depictions of the Stour Valley in his native Suffolk, such as the magnificent painting of *The Vale of Dedham* (1827–8), which was purchased for the National Gallery of Scotland in 1944, with the aid of the National Art Collections Fund. But he also undertook visits to other parts of England, and in October 1835 travelled to Worcester to deliver three lectures on the history of landscape painting for a local learned society. In a letter to the printmaker David

Lucas he declared: 'Who would ever have thought of my turning Methodist preacher, that is, a preacher on "Method" – but I shall do good, to that art for which I live.' He stayed on for a few more days, making drawings, including this study, along the river Severn. It proved to be the last such tour he made.

Pencil on paper · 21.8 × 18.1cm · D 4674
Inscribed by the artist on the verso:
Worcester – 1835
Presented from the collection of Sir Edward Marsh through the National Art Collections Fund
1953

JEAN-AUGUSTE-DOMINIQUE INGRES 1780–1867

Mademoiselle Albertine Hayard (1797–1833)

Ingres, who was the most highly regarded neoclassical painter of the early nineteenth century, was born in Montauban, and studied at the Toulouse Academy before travelling to Paris in 1797. He enjoyed a particularly productive period in Rome (1806–24), where he worked on major paintings for Napoleon, as well as numerous portraits, of which this is a beautiful example. The sitter was the eldest daughter of Charles-Roch Hayard who owned a well known shop that sold artists' materials on the Via dei due Macelli. Ingres was not simply a client, however, as he became a close friend, and created seven portraits of members of the Hayard family. This study is the first in the series and probably shows Albertine at about the age of fourteen, just before her marriage in 1812 to the painter Pierre-Athanse Chauvin; the strict profile format may have been inspired by the contemporary taste for medals, which revived ancient forms of portraiture. Ingres drew Albertine again two years later in an advanced stage of pregnancy (Musée Bonnat, Bayonne). His pencil portraits provided a useful means of supplementing his income, and are characterised by an ability to define details of his sitters' features and clothing with exquisite delicacy. Over 450 such drawings by him survive.

Pencil on paper · 21.5 × 15.1cm · D 5100
Signed and dated, lower left: *Ingres a Rome | 1812*
Purchased with the aid of the National Art Collections Fund 1981

CHRISTEN KØBKE 1810–1848

A View of the Square in the Kastel Looking Towards the Ramparts

Købke is one of the most distinguished of the so-called painters of the Danish Golden Age, whose work represents a brilliant contribution to nineteenth-century European art, although it is not strongly represented in British collections. He started training as an artist at the Royal Academy in Copenhagen in 1822, and from 1828 became a student of C.W. Eckersberg. Købke usually painted small-scale pictures of great precision – landscapes, studies of architectural subjects and portraits of his family and friends. Whatever the subject, he invariably combined carefully observed, often richly coloured naturalistic details, with a sense of controlled abstract design.

This painting was made in about 1830, when he was developing his mature style, and shows the bakery in the Kastel, which is a castle in Copenhagen that served as a prison. The three figures in the foreground are Købke's father, who owned the bakery, Major J.J. Krohn, and the slave Sergeant Spørch (the prisoners were described as 'slaves'). The scene was one with which

Købke was very familiar as he lived within the castle compound from 1817 to 1834. In the later 1830s his family moved out of Copenhagen and he concentrated on depicting more rural scenes; subsequent visits to Germany and Italy broadened the scope of his subject matter still further.

Oil on canvas · 30 × 23.4cm · NG 2505
Purchased with the aid of the National Art Collections Fund 1989

RICHARD DADD 1817–1886
Dancing Jester with Imps

Dadd's intense, idiosyncratic art mirrored his troubled life. He chiefly explored popular strands of Victorian, escapist culture – depicting literary and fairy subjects, and following a trip to the Eastern Mediterranean, orientalist themes. However, on his return to England in 1843 he started to suffer from bouts of insanity, believing himself to be persecuted by demonic powers. He was driven to murder his father, and fled to France, before being captured and confined in Bethlem Hospital and Broadmoor. Sympathetic doctors encouraged him to continue painting and drawing, and he produced images of remarkable complexity and power, which include his portrait of *Sir Alexander Morison* (Scottish National Portrait Gallery) and *The Fairy Feller's Master Stroke* (Tate Britain).

This manic figure is a witty, inventive conceit; the wild quality of his dance is matched by the cacophany of music created by his bells and flute, and the violins and kettledrum played by the imps who accompany him. It can be loosely associated with illustrations Dadd designed for the poem *Robin Goodfellow* – about a mischievous Puck-like figure – which were published as engravings in *The Book of British Ballads* (London, 1842). Artists such as Sir John Tenniel and William Powell Frith also contributed illustrations for this book.

Pen and pencil on paper · 17.7 × 12.8cm · D 4696
Presented from the collection of Sir Edward Marsh through the National Art Collections Fund 1953

GEORGE HENRY 1858–1943
East and West

An elegant Edwardian lady leans forward to study a Japanese figurine; her attitude combines curiosity and condescension. In this simple gesture Henry has encapsulated much of the complex relationship between Britain and Japan which evolved in the nineteenth century, as economic and cultural links between the two nations developed.

An interest in Japan was notably stimulated in Scotland by an exhibition of oriental art in Glasgow's Corporation Galleries in 1882. In that year Henry was studying at Glasgow's School of Art; once he completed his course he worked in a patent office, as a designer of posters, before turning to painting. He visited Japan (1893–4) with his friend and collaborator Edward Atkinson Hornel, and produced numerous studies, chiefly of Japanese women; their travels were partially funded by the great Scottish collector, Sir William Burrell. Later, Henry built a reputation as a fashionable portrait painter in Glasgow and London. Here, he combines the two distinct phases of his work – exhibiting his deft portrait style, which is partly indebted to the work of John Singer Sargent, and his enduring preoccupation with orientalism.

Mr and Mrs Robinson, who lived in Edinburgh and the Borders, built a collection which included the work of a number of the Glasgow Boys, including J.D. Fergusson and F.C.B. Cadell, as well as Henry.

Oil on canvas · 102 × 76.6cm · NG 2454
Signed: *GEORGE HENRY*
Mr and Mrs G.D. Robinson bequest through the National Art Collections Fund 1988

JOSEPH CRAWHALL 1861–1913
The White Drake

Crawhall displays here his ability to imbue a creature with character and nobility, and avoids slipping into the realm of sentimental animal painting, which was explored by so many lesser artists in the nineteenth century. *The White Drake* is an assured exercise in observation, with the dappled, milky light playing across the bird's feathers. It also appeals as an understated and controlled example of formal design, as the daisies and dandelions define the recession of space in the water meadow and create a decorative backdrop with a rich surface pattern.

Crawhall was born in Morpeth in Northumbria, although he is categorised as one of the so-called Glasgow Boys – a group of outstanding and loosely connected young artists who emerged in the 1880s, and came to enjoy an international reputation with their often boldly designed and light-filled compositions. He was particularly associated with two members of the group, E.A. Walton and Arthur Melville, both of whom were also distin-guished watercolourists. A quiet and private man, Crawhall excelled as an observer, particularly of animals, whose companionship he seems to have often preferred to that of humans. According to his sister, he 'loved animals and would not use them for base purposes for he respected their individuality too much'.

Watercolour and gouache on unsized brown linen, laid onto a wood backboard · 41.7 × 59.2cm · D 5415
Signed lower right: *J. Crawhall*
Purchased by Private Treaty with the aid of the Heritage Lottery Fund and the National Art Collections Fund 1996

EXHIBITION CHECKLIST

The drawings and paintings are listed here in chronological order, following the birth dates of artists.

LEONARDO DA VINCI 1452–1519
Studies of a Dog's Paw [recto]

SEE PAGE 14

Metalpoint on paper coated with a pale pink preparation, 14.1 × 10.7cm
Inscribed in black chalk at lower right of recto:
Leonard de V
Purchased by Private Treaty with the aid of the National Art Collections Fund 1991
D 5189
[EDINBURGH ONLY]

RAPHAEL 1483–1520
A Kneeling Nude Woman with her Left Arm Raised

SEE PAGE 16

Red chalk and touches of black chalk over traces of stylus underdrawing on paper, 27.9 × 18.7cm
Purchased by Private Treaty from the Trustees of the Chatsworth Settlement with the aid of the National Heritage Memorial Fund, the Pilgrim Trust, and the National Art Collections Fund 1987
D 5145

AFTER POLIDORO DA CARAVAGGIO 1492–1543
BY AEGIDIUS SADELER I c.1570–c.1609
Designs for Vases

SEE PAGE 18

Engravings on paper, each 24 × 16cm
Purchased by the Patrons of the National Galleries of Scotland with the aid of National Art Collections Fund 1995
P 2911.159 / P 2911.163

MASTER OF THE DIE c.1512–1570
Two Panels of Ornament

Engravings, 21.6 × 16.5cm, 20.8 × 15.1cm
Purchased by the Patrons of the National Galleries of Scotland with the aid of National Art Collections Fund 1995
P2911.167/P2911.168

DENYS CALVAERT c.1540–1619
The Holy Family with the Infant St John the Baptist in a Landscape

SEE PAGE 20

Oil on copper, 42 × 32cm
Purchased with the aid of the Patrons of the National Galleries of Scotland and the National Art Collections Fund 1987
NG 2447

CHRISTOPH SCHWARZ 1548–1592
The Sacrifice of Abraham

Pen and brown ink with some white heightening on paper (squared in black chalk), 16.2 × 26.7cm
Presented by the National Art Collections Fund and the Pilgrim Trust in memory of David, 28th Earl of Crawford and Balcarres 1980
D 5098

GIULIO CESARE PROCACCINI 1574–1625
The Virgin and Child with the Infant St John the Baptist and Attendant Angels

SEE PAGE 22

Oil on panel, 51 × 36.5cm
Purchased with the aid of the Heritage Lottery Fund and the National Art Collections Fund 1995
NG 2647

JOHANN KÖNIG 1586–1642
Angels Escorting Lot and his Family from Sodom

SEE PAGE 24
Gouache on paper laid down on panel, 11.4 × 17.4cm
Purchased with the aid of the National Art Collections
Fund and contributions from two private donors, to mark
the retirement of Keith Andrews as Keeper of Prints and
Drawings (1958–1985) 1985
D 5137

NICOLAS POUSSIN 1594–1665
A Dance to the Music of Time

SEE PAGE 26
Pen and brown ink and traces of black chalk on paper,
14.8 × 19.9cm
Purchased by Private Treaty with the aid of the
National Art Collections Fund, the Pilgrim Trust, the
Edith M. Ferguson Bequest, and contributions from two
private donors 1984
D 5127
[LONDON ONLY]

GOFFREDO WALS *c*.1595–*c*.1638
Landscape with Christ and St Peter

SEE PAGE 28
Oil on copper, 28.5cm (diameter)
Purchased with the aid of the National Art Collections
Fund 1990
NG 2516

PIETRO DA CORTONA 1596–1669
St Ivo Intervening on Behalf of the Poor

Black chalk and grey wash heightened with white on light
brown paper (squared in black chalk), 43.3 × 30.7cm
Purchased with the aid of the National Heritage Memorial
Fund and the National Art Collections Fund 1992
D 5327

REMBRANDT 1606–1669
Ecce Homo: Christ Presented to the People

Drypoint, 38.3 × 45.5cm
Accepted in lieu of tax and allocated through the National
Art Collections Fund 1992
P 2878

PIETRO TESTA 1612–1650
The Massacre of the Innocents

Pen and ink over red chalk on paper, 25.2 × 36.4cm
Purchased with the aid of the National Art Collections
Fund 1973
D 4993

PAUL ANDROUET DU CERCEAU
c.1630–1710
Designs for Friezes with Acanthus Foliage

Engravings, 18 × 29cm; 18.8 × 28.5cm
Purchased by the Patrons of the National Galleries of
Scotland with the aid of National Art Collections Fund
1995
P 2911.131 / P 2911.134

CIRO FERRI 1634?–1689
The Meeting of St Francis and St Dominic

Red and black chalk, heightened with white (partly
oxidised) on paper, 25.9 × 39cm
Purchased with the aid of the Foundation for Sport and
the Arts and the National Art Collections Fund 1992
D 5337

SEBASTIANO RICCI 1659–1734
Christ Healing the Blind Man

SEE PAGE 30
Oil on canvas, 52 × 67.5cm
Purchased with the aid of the National Art Collections
Fund 1994
NG 2623

PIERRE SUBLEYRAS 1699–1749
The Crucifixion of St Peter

Oil on canvas, 46.7 × 31cm
Purchased with the aid of the National Art Collections
Fund 1995
NG 2635

RICHARD WILSON 1713?–1782
Temple of the Sibyl, Tivoli

Black and white chalk on paper prepared with a brown
wash, 24.8 × 41cm

Presented from the collection of Sir Edward Marsh
through the National Art Collections Fund 1953
D 4667

GEORGE ROMNEY 1734–1802
Study for 'Elizabeth Warren as Hebe'

SEE PAGE 32
Pen, ink, and wash on paper, 30.9 × 21cm
Presented from the collection of Sir Edward Marsh
through the National Art Collections Fund 1953
D 4651

THOMAS ROWLANDSON 1756–1827
Studying the Flesh Tints: Rubens Setting his Palette

Pen and watercolour on paper, 19.9 × 18.2cm
Presented from the collection of Sir Edward Marsh
through the National Art Collections Fund 1953
D 4671

WILLIAM BLAKE 1757–1827
Job Confessing his Presumption to God who Answers from the Whirlwind

SEE PAGE 34
Pen and ink and watercolour over pencil on paper,
39.3 × 33cm
Signed, lower left: *W B inv.*
Presented by the Trustees of Mr Graham Robertson
through the National Art Collections Fund 1949
D 2117

ALEXANDER NASMYTH 1758–1840
A View of Tantallon Castle with the Bass Rock

SEE PAGE 36
Oil on canvas, 92 × 122.3cm
Inscribed and signed with initials
Purchased with the aid of the National Art Collections
Fund 1994
NG 2627

FRANÇOIS-XAVIER FABRE 1766–1837
Portrait of a Man

SEE PAGE 38
Oil on canvas, 61.5 × 50cm
Signed and dated 1809

Purchased with the aid of the National Art Collections
Fund 1992
NG 2548

JOSEPH MALLORD WILLIAM TURNER 1775–1851
Heriot's Hospital, Edinburgh

SEE PAGE 40
Watercolour on paper, 16.6 × 25cm
Purchased with the aid of the Heritage Lottery Fund and
the National Art Collections Fund 1988
D 5447

THOMAS GIRTIN 1775–1802
The Village of Jedburgh, Roxburgh

SEE PAGE 42
Watercolour over pencil on paper, 30.2 × 52.1cm
Signed and dated in brown watercolour, lower left
corner: *Girtin 1800*
Purchased with the aid of funds from the National
Heritage Memorial Fund, the Pilgrim Trust, and the
National Art Collections Fund 1988
D 5175

JOHN CONSTABLE 1776–1837
View on the River Severn at Worcester

SEE PAGE 44
Pencil on paper, 21.8 × 18.1cm
Inscribed by the artist on the verso: *Worcester – 1835*
Presented from the collection of Sir Edward Marsh
through the National Art Collections Fund 1953
D 4674

JEAN-AUGUSTE-DOMINIQUE INGRES 1780–1867
Mademoiselle Albertine Hayard (1797–1833)

SEE PAGE 46
Pencil on paper, 21.5 × 15.1cm
Signed and dated, lower left: *Ingres a Rome/1812*
Purchased with the aid of the National Art Collections
Fund 1981
D 5100

JOHN SELL COTMAN 1782–1842

The Coming Storm

Watercolour on paper, 17.4 × 25.3cm
Presented from the collection of Sir Edward Marsh
through the National Art Collections Fund 1953
D 4697

DAVID COX 1783–1859

A Farm Building

Watercolour on paper, 20.7 × 27cm
Presented from the collection of Sir Edward Marsh
through the National Art Collections Fund 1953
D 4698

DAVID WILKIE 1785–1841

The Wool Spinner

Black chalk and watercolour on paper, 17.4 × 25.8cm
Presented from the collection of Sir Edward Marsh
through the National Art Collections Fund 1953
D 4688

EMILIUS DITLEV BAERENTZEN
1799–1868

The Winther Family

Oil on canvas, 70.5 × 65.5cm
Purchased with the aid of the Patrons of the National
Galleries of Scotland and the National Art Collections
Fund 1987
NG 2451

CHRISTEN KØBKE 1810–1848

*A View of the Square in the Kastel Looking Towards
the Ramparts*

SEE PAGE 48
Oil on canvas, 30 × 23.4cm
Purchased with the aid of the National Art Collections
Fund 1989
NG 2505

CHRISTEN KØBKE 1810–1848

Portrait of Cecilia Margrete Købke

Oil on canvas, 23.5 × 19.5
Purchased with the aid of the National Art Collections
Fund 2002
NG 2741

RICHARD DADD 1817–1886

Dancing Jester with Imps

SEE PAGE 50
Pen and pencil on paper, 17.7 × 12.8cm
Presented from the collection of Sir Edward Marsh
through the National Art Collections Fund 1953
D N4696

GEORGE HENRY 1858–1943

East and West

SEE PAGE 52
Oil on canvas, 102 × 76.6cm
Signed: *GEORGE HENRY*
Mr and Mrs G.D. Robinson bequest through the
National Art Collections Fund 1988
NG 2454

JOSEPH CRAWHALL 1861–1913

The White Drake

SEE PAGE 54
Watercolour and gouache on unsized brown linen, laid
onto a wood backboard, 41.7 × 59.2cm
Signed lower right: *J. Crawhall*
Purchased by Private Treaty with the aid of the Heritage
Lottery Fund and the National Art Collections Fund
1996
D 5415

DAVID GAULD 1865–1936

St Agnes

Oil on canvas, 61.3 × 35.5
Purchased with the aid of the National Art Collections
Fund 1999
NG 2701

FURTHER READING

Much of the information in this book is drawn from other National Gallery of Scotland publications, which should be referred to for fuller discussions of the paintings and drawings:

Michael Clarke, et al., *The Draughtsman's Art: Master Drawings from the National Gallery of Scotland*, exh. cat., National Gallery of Scotland, Edinburgh 1999

Michael Clarke, et al., *A Companion Guide to the National Gallery of Scotland*, Edinburgh 2000

Timothy Clifford, et al., *Raphael: The Pursuit of Perfection*, exh. cat., National Gallery of Scotland, Edinburgh 1994

Timothy Clifford, et al., *Designs of Desire: Architectural and Ornament Prints and Drawings 1500–1850*, exh. cat., National Gallery of Scotland, Edinburgh 1999

Hugh Macandrew, *Old Master Drawings from the National Gallery of Scotland*, exh. cat., National Gallery of Art, Washington DC 1990

Katrina Thomson, *Turner and Walter Scott: The Provincial Antiquities and Picturesque scenery of Scotland*, exh. cat., National Gallery of Scotland, Edinburgh 1999

Saved for Scotland, Works of Art Acquired with the Help of the National Art Collections Fund, exh. cat., National Gallery of Scotland, Edinburgh 1991

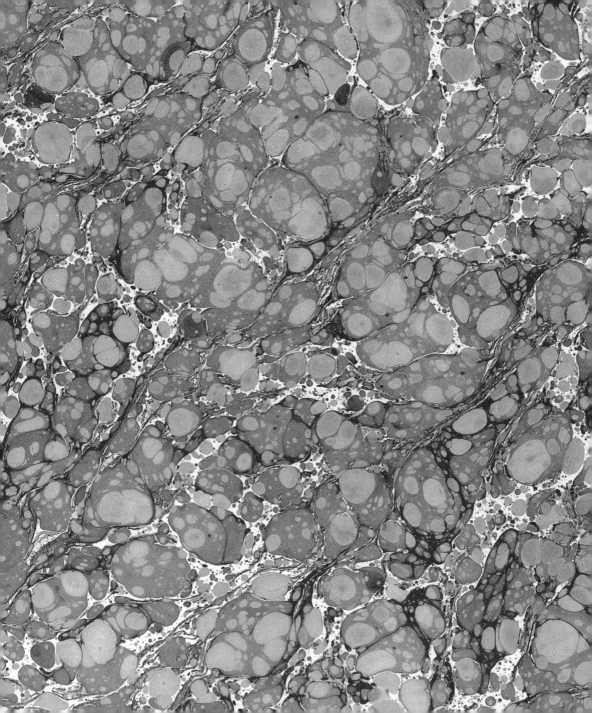